Muse

CRAB ORCHARD AWARD SERIES IN POETRY

Muse

Susan Aizenberg

For Dave —
with heartfelt
admiration &
thanks —
fondly,
Susan
8/2/05
Omaha

Crab Orchard Review

&

Southern Illinois University Press

CARBONDALE AND EDWARDSVILLE

Printed in the United States of America

05   04   03   02   4   3   2   1

The Crab Orchard Award Series in Poetry is a joint publishing venture
of Southern Illinois University Press and *Crab Orchard Review*. This
series has been made possible by the generous support of the Office
of the President of Southern Illinois University and the Office of the
Vice Chancellor for Academic Affairs and Provost at Southern Illinois
University Carbondale.

Crab Orchard Award Series in Poetry Editor: Jon Tribble
Judge for 2001: Maura Stanton

Library of Congress Cataloging-in-Publication Data
Aizenberg, Susan.
    Muse / Susan Aizenberg.
        p. cm.—(Crab Orchard award series in poetry)
    I. Title. II. Series.
PS3601.I94 M87 2002
811'.6—dc21
ISBN 0-8093-2443-1 (pbk. : alk. paper)   2001047839

The paper used in this publication meets the minimum requirements of
American National Standard for Information Sciences—Permanence of
Paper for Printed Library Materials, ANSI Z39.48-1992. ♾

for Aaron, Christopher, and Jeffrey Aizenberg

The tumult in the heart
keeps asking questions.
And then it stops and undertakes to answer
in the same tone of voice.
No one could tell the difference.
—Elizabeth Bishop
"Four Poems"

Contents

Acknowledgments xi

One   White Cat and Notebook: A Still Life 3

Two   Contrast, Composition 9
Nights Mutable as Water Revise Themselves into the
    Shape of Our Extravagant Past 11
What It Is 12
Cortland, 1970 14
Twenty-Five Years from Anywhere Like That 15
Kiss 16
For the Dark Girl 18
Triptych: For Michael 19
In the Frame 22
Far Rockaway 23
Debut: Late Lines for a Thirtieth Birthday 25
The Uses of Metaphor 27
Grand Street 28
Against Romance 30
Muse 31

Three   Three Poems for Judi 37
The Life You Really Have 39
Memory from Childhood 41
Luminous Child 42
Flying West 43
Art 45
Ode for My Son at Seventeen 47
Half-Light: No Feeling 48
Sometimes When You're Asleep 49
Heat 51
Georgic on Waking 53
L'Heure Bleue 54
Grace 56
Florigraphy 58
Prayer 60

Notes 63

Acknowledgments

Grateful acknowledgment is made to the editors of the following publications, in which poems in this collection have appeared, sometimes in slightly different form or with different titles:

AGNI—"Nights Mutable as Water Revise Themselves into the Shape of Our Extravagant Past"
Alaska Quarterly Review—"Prayer," "Ward in Chancery" from "Muse"
Baybury Review—"Contrast, Composition"
Chelsea—"White Cat and Notebook: A Still Life," "Against Romance"
Connecticut Review—"Heat," "Half-Light: No Feeling"
Crab Orchard Review—"Florigraphy," "Ode for My Son at Seventeen"
Devil's Millhopper—"Grand Street"
thedrunkenboat.com—"Memory from Childhood"
ForPoetry.com—"Far Rockaway"
The Journal—"The Life You Really Have," "Georgic on Waking," "Three Poems for Judi"
Kalliope—"Debut: Late Lines for a Thirtieth Birthday"
Laurel Review—"Flying West"
Omaha Metropolitan—"The Uses of Metaphor"
ONTHEBUS—"Twenty-Five Years from Anywhere Like That"
Philadelphia Inquirer—"The Rim" from "Muse"
Poetry Miscellany—"What It Is"
Prague Review—"Twenty-Five Years from Anywhere Like That"
Prairie Schooner—"In the Frame," *"L'Heure Bleue,"* "For the Dark Girl," "Kiss"
Spoon River Poetry—"Sometimes When You're Asleep"
SunDog—"Art"
Third Coast—"Luminous Child"

The poem "Muse" was first published as a limited edition, fine arts press chapbook (Nosila Press, 1998). My thanks to Alison Wilson.

"Florigraphy" first appeared as a letterpress broadside (BradyPress, 2000). Thanks to Denise Brady.

Thanks, too, to Maura Stanton, Jon Tribble, and the folks at *Crab Orchard Review* and Southern Illinois University Press; to the Nebraska Arts Council, for two fellowships that helped with the completion of this book; to the English department at Creighton University; and to Fiona McCrae and Anne Czarnecki at Graywolf Press and series editor Askold Melnyczuk, who first published a number of these poems in *Take Three/2: AGNI New Poets Series* (Graywolf Press, 1997).

Finally, my heartfelt gratitude to the many generous friends whose support and careful readings of these poems have made this book and so much more possible, especially Erin Belieu, Art Homer, Carol-Lynn Marrazzo, Betsy Sholl, Pamela Stewart, Belle Waring, and David Wojahn; to my brother, Michael David, for first showing me the way, and to Jeffrey, Christopher, and Aaron Aizenberg.

One

White Cat and Notebook: A Still Life

. . . I seem to be able to tell what objects are important
to me by what tends to stay in the picture as it develops.
—Richard Diebenkorn

Rain hushes this February morning,
that same infusing chill

that once entered the slim bones
of your hands until they ached, flushed

and swollen joints another
of your body's betrayals; that laved

the grit of your radiant cities, brassy
asphalt fragrance rising, mnemonic,

off the charged streets, minor chords
of your unappeasable ghosts

laddering its scent on the weather.
Here, this small midwestern

city's muffled in winter's cottony greys,
the landlocked sky impassive

as the calendar squares telling these
mortal days' inexorable slide

to the anniversary I refuse to mark
in. For hours I've been reading

theories of painting, how the dulled
edges of kitchen knives, poppies

fading in a glass, a frayed jacket, resolve
to *surrogates for the figure, signs*

3

of figural absence denoting presence . . .
summoning your Chicago rooms I've known

only in letters, the coruscating poems
you called *these notes to myself,*

imagining objects you once touched,
for a still life I might paint for you.

> *Still life, in Diebenkorn's interpretation . . . is the pro-*
> *cess of creating an intense unity from which everything*
> *dispensable has been removed because the pressure of*
> *feeling required it. . . . Parts have to be assembled, of*
> *course, before some can be removed.*
>
> —John Elderfield, *Figure and Field*

I can plot them on a canvas
in my mind: the yellowed dressmaker's

dummy, straight-pins piercing
the bird-down slope of breast, shape

rounded as Monroe's, behind it the window
through which you watched blown skies

mapped with billboards and spiked
antennas, fading rose contrails, frame

for the El's sparking tracks echoing
the mannequin's curves, the question mark

lines of the white cat preening
on the sill. I can sketch a scarred deal

table, circa 1930, in the foreground,
on it, creamy gouache of a highball glass

perspiring beside pill bottles, their labels
rough white strokes, a few pointillist

dots of prescription type; behind them,
a notebook, snake of rubber tubing

coiled, toxic, in the slumbering kit. But no.
Four years now since I got the call.

Louise could not repeat what I could not
bear to hear: *say it again, say it again,*

I sang, hoarse cuckoo with my mainspring
come wildly unsprung.

> *. . . represented forms are loaded with psychological
> feeling. It can't ever be* just painting.
> —Richard Diebenkorn

Four years and still the images break down.
Lynda, I don't know what I believe

about where you are now, or whether
my words dissolve like mist

in etherous air. I can't conjure you
among these scumbled layers: clusters

of family photos, a translucent bride
in overpainted silk and fedora, cherries

a slash of ruby pigment darkening
the brim: can't find you in the gleam

of aluminum crutches reflecting
off the illusion of her captured face.

Details fail to coalesce. But the carmine
and silver amulet box you sent me

from Cuba—*when you lose your faith,
take mine for you,* on lavender tissue—

still blesses my desk, whispers it's not folly
to believe that once, months beyond

your death, I felt the heat of your living
arm shawl my shoulders. Teacher,

even if it's true elegy's fated
to be most about the living, pictures,

always, to be first the story of the painter's
subjective eye, I'll complete this one

for you, paint out *everything dispensable*
till all that remains is the ivory cat,

your sleek familiar, like Hermes
beside the window, and the open notebook;

paint in a wash of violet
for your elegantly scrawled lines.

Two

Contrast, Composition

I don't know what color to name Ray's tree.
Perhaps it's one of the *broken and neutral,* nameless
colors Van Gogh believed were *the foundation of everything.*
Perhaps not. All morning I've been reading

Van Gogh's letters, returning to his discussions
of color and descriptions of scenes he will paint.
Along the quays at Antwerp, he takes a *fruitful walk,*
where all he sees—a muddy white horse

beside a warehouse, Flemish sailors laughing
in their beers, a Chinese girl with *a small, oval face*—
offers itself as contrast and composition
beneath a grey sky. *One could undertake everything here,*

he tells Theo. This is not so many years
before the *good god sun,* the *devil of a mistral,*
the radiant days and electric nights at Arles, where
he discovers the sunflower, *somewhat my own,*

and where he will paint his first, brilliant
version of *The Starry Night.* Not so many years
before his neighbors will petition to have him
confined. *I am well just now,* he writes

from the asylum, *except for a certain undercurrent
of vague sadness.* Here, the late-twentieth
century light clarifies a composition perfectly
American: beyond Ray's and mine, similar

houses. One bears a wind-rippled flag,
another a canary-yellow ribbon snaked around its
mailbox post in support of our most recent
war. I don't know if Van Gogh would have painted

this or how much one can undertake
among these wood and glass and brick façades
that give nothing away, these neighbors out
or lost behind drawn curtains. Perhaps

he'd have done this sky the faint blue
of fresh milk, these laddering sparrows drawing
the eye to Our Lady of Mercy's steeple rising
white, narrow as a spike, toward an idea of Paradise.

Nights Mutable as Water Revise Themselves into the Shape of Our Extravagant Past

so that even the mildest gesture
astonishes, just as this night's fickle
snowfall startles the ripening orchard,

throngs of Cortland dwarfs, rimed
in silver, curving their slim branches
to dark earth. Trailing our rockiest

good intentions, that slipshod
cortège of poor elections and risky
marriages, we hurtled, breakneck,

toward a future dubious as any history
text. And maybe we were liars,
crooning blue lullabies as we battled

for purchase, ambitious for anything
costly, even these small, moony apples—
charming but wrong.

What It Is

Absent—that was what he was: so absent from everything most
densely real and near to those about him that it sometimes
startled him to find they still imagined he was there.
  —Edith Wharton, *The Age of Innocence*

All morning the wind suggests
departure, troubling
the glass, ferrying the dead

leaves, lavish in their traveling
colors, from branch to gutter
as it makes for distant latitudes.

And it's erotic, isn't it—
the way it shifts, fickle, hushed
as an insinuating gesture,

among the lightening trees?
Maybe it's this novel I've been reading,
Wharton's Archer so *absent*

he's like a newborn, astonished
by anything—light sparking
off cut crystal, the cool timbre

of a woman's low voice.
And I must admit it scares me
to know so well those shadow

rooms he's cluttered with imaginary
furniture, what it is to bring
to them his cherished books

and company, to wait with him,
beneath a Paris sky the bluest
glacier could get lost in, losing

my place to this insistent wind,
until dusk, evening's resplendent pardon.

Cortland, 1970

Always Monday, light October drizzle
misting our hair, wet-
wool musk of our peacoats.
Remember your father's library?
Three-for-a-buck novels,

all the rosy *headlights*
he could dream, group-gropes he couldn't.
Breakfast was beer in a jelly
glass. Then the ten-block walk,
hardscrabble shacks

imploding, to swing shift
at Smith Corona. I still have the scar
acid etched through my jeans
that first night. Peeling them down
in the ladies' room, I found a black

circle the size of a quarter.
In May we married between small claims
and traffic courts, my mother
sweating in cheap mink, the best man
sniffling, aching to get straight.

Twenty-Five Years from Anywhere Like That

Shoulder, hip, and heel, I sprint
faster in my wingless Nikes, circling the Boys Town
track as Bonnie Raitt's roadhouse wail
and slide guitar snake wire.

Cottonwoods blur like a hypnotist's
watch until the track disappears and I'm back
in the third row of the Fillmore East,
where Janis Joplin, too wasted

to sing, slugged honeyed mash
from a high-tipped bottle. We sang "Ball & Chain"
a cappella on the D train, grinding
high notes breaking the national anthem

as the subway rocked the sour dark,
red and blue lights strobing.
That year, we traded up to barefoot rides
in limousines, four-way sunshine

for breakfast: onion grass
looney-tuning into little green men.
Now teenage girls from Boys Town pass me
quick, a middle-aged woman

they can't imagine seventeen, running away,
that burnt-out place
on Rickard Street, a bare mattress under
the corona of shotgun holes

left there for the landlord
by a flute player who cared for no one
but sent his clear notes
up the fire escape anyway.

Kiss

And when the moment,
  like an overdue train bearing to us
    someone loved and too long

      gone, a train we've waited days
      and nights for, pacing the platform,
    our pulses thrumming *when, when,*

arrives—the camera close up, lush
  sweep of strings, *adagio,* the light high key,
    resplendent as the dew-rinsed,

      saturated, dizzyingly green panoramas
  the cinematographer's mapped as Camelot—
      the moment

we have waited for, with the lovers,
  since their first meeting, Guinevere crouched
    among damp reeds, unafraid, despite

her torn dress, smiling as she watches—
  he's young, all muscle and wit, a man's
    easy grace—smiling, too, despite the chain

and mail–clad villains, the honed,
  bloody swords, knight of girlhood's promise,
    you remember—that moment

    when the camera frames the kiss
she's asked him, finally, for. They are not tender,
but open their mouths wide, so we think

      of eating, their heads working,
      a kind of fever, love's other face—
        we recognize it, don't we? Lancelot,

the man, the archetypal *only, always,*
        we dreamt of as girls those rainy childhood
        afternoons, Kens and Barbies moving

        stiffly in our small hands, our mothers'
   stolen stilettos gorgeously tripping us up.
   It's that kiss you want for so long

        that when you take it you take it
        greedy as a thief and always with as much payment
   due. And we want them to go on,

though we know the ending, that the camera
        must pan to a three-shot, Arthur's ragged
        face. We want them to go past

what they — and we — can bear, to follow
        his head gentle down her neck, her mouth
        against his bare shoulder. We want the music

        to swell, lavish, hokey, romance
   engulfing us like some over-sweet perfume,

                so wholly our lives
        become epic, a kiss worth whatever it costs.

For the Dark Girl

If you can get through the twilight, you'll live through the night.
    —Dorothy Parker

In furnished rooms drab as offices, she wakes
at dusk—a habit, though it's twenty years
too late for drinks at Tony Soma's, too late
for the numbing rounds, sunrise at Polly Adler's.
A Red Label eye-opener soothes *the rams,*
though the city below's become another failed
romance, its darkening, storied streets one more home
she's lost the key to. Another shot to quell
her head's clamor—memory like some drunken
guest who won't shut up or leave. Rain thrums
in enervated measure on the glass, sweetens
the ruined air. She breathes its chill perfume,
tells her daily rosary: *Dear God in Heaven,*
O Please—make me stop writing like a woman.

Triptych: For Michael

My brother wakes at forty
on a solitary couch, slipped from comfort,

night's black shawl, his wife
and child adrift in rooms beyond

him, remote as stars
in the separate constellations

of their sleep. He's dreamed himself
as ravenous ghost, rises

to work—a self-portrait, the life-
sized cropping of his head doubled

on two panels. Such an intricate
and fraught choreography

as he pours the heated wax, its gold
fire veiling the image,

the image fading, a thickening
shroud obscuring, not quite revealing,

the other he seeks—and now the spilled wax—
his timing, for a moment, off—

its livid glove fused to his naked
hand. He must hold it, radiant with pain,

all night out the window, twelve
stories above Manhattan,

a small nova releasing
its human heat into the city's chill air.

———

Even as a child he sought
the fishable spot, a sleepwalker's faith
in the invisible drawing him

through the fertile dark
of our apartment, past the fixed
pole of our dreaming parents,

and once, out to the moon-soaked
street, so that, always, after,
the doors were double-locked.

I'd wake to fevered whispers,
him telling the beads of whatever vision
he'd shaped from the day, one arm

raised, a small divining rod,
as if already he knew a stream of secrets
roiled beneath us, dopplegangers

twinned our smiling, daylight selves.

———

Beespun yellow alchemized to savage
   red, black hole black, the queasy green of decay
or money—*painting's like sex,*
   he says, at twenty means falls of molten wax

melded to six-foot swastikas, crosses,
   gritty punk stars he's layered to resemble
human flesh, reptilian skin, ocean, sky.
   Now it's faces and bodies that arrest

him, human icons the objects he must return
   to. He weds to them their second,
muslin skins, until they're shadow and question
   beneath wax cauls, luminous and mute

as angels are, as Michael, for a moment,
   is—see how he's held in the forgiving
half-light of the studio's oily haze,
   their messenger, object of their calm regard.

In the Frame

after Hopper

Instead of the blonde, I'd paint my mother.
The sunlit dress can stay. Her hat and shadow
mean she's growing impatient,
and though her face says nothing, I know my
father's putting everything down
on a long shot, late.

I'd keep the limestone façade
behind her, the amber-lit hall where my grandmother
pushes her janitor's mop and pail
along the staircase, her hands reddening
in ammonia. The blowsy
curtain marks my mother's bedroom,
bare dresser and narrow bed.

Younger than I am now, she can't
know the years of seasonal migrations, a wingless
bird behind the tinted windshield,
following horse trailers between Aqueduct
and Hialeah. She'll wait for hours
in the stark light of Hopper's summer evening,
and even if I wanted to, I couldn't
paint her rising.

Far Rockaway

Look: a man is teaching his children to ride
the big waves. Hand in hand in hand they wade out

past the first mild breakers. Icy green fingers
tap the children's thin chests. Rising on their toes,

they inch forward, through the sea's startling
gradations: blue green, bottle green, ink pad

blue, violet—until, peering down, they see only
the plunging dark. Sea lettuce and jellyfish swirl

past them. Sun jewels the far surfaces, where a trawler
chugs, placid as a great blue, along the horizon.

Cormorants and gulls carve their elegant wheelies
in the bleached August sky, their shrieks another thread

in the day's tapestry of sounds: the insect drone
of a Piper Cub trailing its banner, *Noxema Cools Skin Burn,*

overhead, the tide's iambic susurrus. Now, somewhere
deep, past the quivering red buoys, the vast machine

that runs the ocean cranks up, and it's as if the girl
can hear the rusty gears, the ferrous clank of metal,

as the first line gathers and rolls toward them, the waves
rising, immense and black, swells laced with churning

froth, as the sea shifts its great weight, slowly, at first,
and then bursts towards shore, the three small figures watching.

The man laughs, and the children laugh, with pleasure
and fear. For years the girl will dream of this wild coast,

a single wave screening the sky, a *tsunami*, swollen
with intent, that chases her upshore, crashing through the seawall

so she must run, breathless, for home, the fierce water
relentless behind her as some furious ghost, her name etched

in salt graffitying dank alley walls. But now she waits,
letting it come, as her father has taught her, her lips

bluing, goose pimples roughening her skin, seasoaked
until she feels as if she might be turning back through history,

that chilled enough, they might sprout gills and fins,
devolve to the watery start. The enormous wave looms,

suspended like held breath above them, and they dive
low, into its dark curl, trusting the surge to pass over them,

that they will surface to calm, the ocean rocking gently now,
spent wash foaming its delicate palimpsest along the shore.

Debut: Late Lines for a Thirtieth Birthday

Adoptees do not have the luxury of envisioning their celebrated births. . . . they often
know nothing of their debuts. . . .
   —Jan L. Waldron, *Giving Away Simone*

You say you can't sleep nights, imagining them,
   the wayward girls of Omaha, Nebraska, 1965,
the chill green rooms of Booth Charity Hospital bare
   as cloister cells, where they'll labor hard—*learn*

their lesson, the doctor says—and leave the infants
   they may name but not hold. It's the weekly outing
that gets you. Movies the Junior League springs for,
   something sweet at Dairy Queen, how, docile

as calves, they're led in line by twos, a few holding
   hands like the schoolgirls they are. But look—here's
your mother, the copper hair she'll pass to you
   mirroring the late September sun, that same glamour-

puss mole etched on the still soft curve of her cheek.
   She won't line up, doesn't want ice cream, waits
outside, slouched against a red Mustang she'd like
   to own, smoking the Old Golds she knows say

bad girl, even now. Along the empty street,
   this part of town where no one comes, the first leaves
drop to skitter along the gutter, make her think
   of snow, of the movie they've just seen—Lean's

Zhivago and Lara warm with vodka and lovemaking
   in a glistening blizzard of a house, snow veiling everything,
the gas lamps and satin couches, even the poet's desk
   slick with frost, of their lost daughter, how years

later, she refuses the proferred gift of her past.
No Slavic romance in your mother's past,
just some west Nebraska town so small it's no more
   than a stutter in the long silence of the prairie,

her father's strap, regular as church once she began
   to show, the pursed mouth of her mother, a Greyhound
into this dirty city, where for days she slept and read
   from a book of names, choosing *Helen* for you,

maybe thinking of those thousand ships, maybe
   of some favorite teacher, one who called her writing
good. You can't know any of this, anymore than she knows
   it's just hours from your birth. I like to think you'll arrive

through a shared dream of iced and glittering Russian
   trees, Yuri smiling at the first sun he's seen in months
before turning to his work, that you debut to a welcoming
   chorus of *troika* bells and *balalaikas,* a cry of wolves.

The Uses of Metaphor

after reading the *Amnesty International Report on Torture*

They call themselves *doctors,* speak
of *taking the submarine, the plane
ride, dragon's chair, the parrot.*
They call it *the putting of the question,
Civic therapy. A spiritual séance. Collective
training.* At night they look into the faces
of their children. They touch the soft
bodies of their wives. Turning up their radios,
their ears fat with cotton, they pretend
to hear nothing. Only the language
of their dreams is literal. All night the alphabet
moves behind their eyes. Their tongues
work in their mouths, forming and re-forming
the words *water, electricity, blood.*

What if one Sunday morning on the Lower East Side,
Christmas shoppers from Scarsdale
bundled in mink, their mouths bright with lipstick,
swirled, chattering like children
released from school, on their way to bargains
and light lunches, up the steep concrete
entrance to the IRT, past a woman swaying
barefoot on the top step, wayward hair
swinging over her closed eyes as she rocked
precariously backward, her ribs
and cold-hardened nipples showing through a thin
nylon wrap, wailing, mournful as a bird,
a man's name you think may be *B-o-b-b-b-y*, *B-o-b-b-b-y*,
her speech too slurred for you to be sure?
What if your friend, no tourist like you, steered
you by one elbow through the perfumed air
trailed by the shoppers, saying, *nothing we can do,*
she'd probably spit in our faces? Would you
imagine you knew the lives of those women,
console yourself with clichés of Valium
and infidelities, discontented sons and daughters
like your friend, and you, and maybe (thinking
you'd discovered some irony) like the woman
parting them easily as a traffic cop,
so gone she's made all of you invisible?
Wouldn't you still exclaim over mushroom loaf
and mashed potatoes at the famous dairy restaurant,
laughing at the comic waiters, their accents
like your grandfather's as they tell you
what to order? What if your friend pointed
out the beauty of the young girl working
the register, how she resembled a green-eyed,
bored madonna, handling the keys
and customers to the same narcotic rhythm
as the woman keening on the subway steps, the traffic
cop rocking on his heels at the intersection,

holding herself the way the shoppers will hold their bags
all the way to Scarsdale, the way you
will hold your friend's arm as you walk back
past the IRT, where no one will be
crying for Bobby; wouldn't you agree, saying,
Yes, she is a beauty, I can see that, yes?

Against Romance

Mariano puts his mouth to the alto, coming in,
smooth as smoke and aged bourbon,

on *I X Love*, a tune, Mingus says,
he wrote for *my ex-love, a love I x-x-x-ed out*,

and the shape of the sound his breath
makes is the sway of strangers slow-dancing

in a *noir* film, a sexual haze turning them
glamorous, though her dress is shabby, his suit

too large or small. Now Mingus swings
in, and the music's narcotic, a drifting weave

of memory and imagination, the film a waking
dream, unspooling, languid, in our minds.

The couple presses in to one another, not
moving their feet, in no hurry to begin

or end their brief story. We're hoping for passion,
that the room they'll reach will be clean, gently

lit, their lovemaking tender. But the tune refuses
what's sentimental, and we know their loneliness

is not enough to bind them, though they cling
as if they could become a single body

or as if they might leave their bodies entirely.

Muse

—Vivienne Eliot, 1889–1947

Tom's Bloomsbury bunch called her 'the river girl.' They were afraid of her . . .
—Maurice Haigh-Wood

She has everything to give that I want, and she gives it.
—T. S. Eliot

I. RIVER GIRL
a litany

Incarnate provocation
　　　bag of ferrets　flirt

　　　　morally insane, frivolous

a silly little woman
attractive to men but not a girl
　　to bring to Mother

　　　　shallow self-centered
　　　　a prima dona

preoccupied with romance, gross
　　with women's troubles

　　　　that torture
　　　　reeking of ether
her voice a shriek—

（it's true she chose her men poorly:
a lover who found her *hellish, loathsome,*
her genius husband
with his truss, his vow of celibacy,
his green face powder
and stained lips. Her own face *white,*

mottled from an excess of bromide,
her eyes vague, acutely sad).

1905, April

                    Delicious, this absence of pain—

On the smooth pitch behind Father's
house, the adults linger over cricket. She hears

   the soft knock of wood,
      low murmurs, laughter.

         Inside Martha scrubs
   this morning's bloody sheets, another
      ruined lace gown. For once she doesn't care.

   Her head light, gut
      unclenched, she sways

past the rhododendron sentries, drifts,

         invisible, it seems, across the meadow's
         riotous gorse, wild red vetch,
white stitchwort, pink ladysmock.

         She thinks the flowers may be speaking.

         Bless Dr. Arnold, bless Mother.

Bless most of all those bottles gleaming
      on the bedstand, their strange names—*anodyne, bromide*—
         lovely as the names of flowers.

      She moves deep into the woods' damp
shade, until she's lost

in blues—
violet, aquamarine, gentian, cobalt . . .

Endymion nonscriptus—bluebells.

Sodden leaves and these many
silent, soothing bells erase
the footpath, and because she's sixteen,

her head cloudy with ether
and alcohol, she feels she's floating
on azure, a magic carpet

that might take her anywhere. It's so quiet now
she can hear the lisp of grass snakes,

each bird calling, the hush
and chirr of morning gossip
passing, neighborly,

among the sheltering larch.

3. WARD IN CHANCERY
what they took from her

Photographs she'd lived with twenty years, her husband's love letters.
Trunks of filmy scarves, sheer, petal-colored dresses. Her lacework.
Pairs of pastel boots with their many pearl buttons, those straw hats
pinned with gleaming fruit, stockings the color of sorbet—even her
fascist drag, black waistcoat and cape, the ivory cigarette holder. They
took her passport, her driver's license, her right to vote or appeal for
release. They took her powders and elixirs, her car keys, the keys to her
flat. Her money. Her mother lined a steamer with silk pillows, packed
her diaries and sheet music, the hinged box of watercolors, satin-toed
dancing shoes she'd worn down at the heels, French scent T. hated for
its *female masking* trick. They took her books, cartoons she'd drawn, the
stories and poems she'd written, her copies of *The Criterion*, the margins
scrawled with purple-inked comments in her spidery hand.

4. THE RIM
Northumberland House
1947, January

Reflexed and crownlike, happy enough
    in the drawing room's dim afternoon light,
the cyclamen's petals bloom, pink
    as nursery paper, above its mottled leaves—
a ring of hearts the damp, sober green
    of moss. These fugitive winter days

reluctant darkness shudders into morning,
    resolves, each twilight, into evening's
phantom vacancies. In between, the tea
    kettle's fading hiss, this cloying scent
of hothouse flowers. I watch snow ghosting
    the patio, the abandoned gazebo,

woodsmoke rising over the silver birches
    to brindle a chalky sky. I watch myself
moving, like a wraith, between the armchair
    and the window, between this overheated
room, its moldering velvets and aging damasks,
    these yellowed doilies we residents stitch,

and every feverish, echoing room sprung
    from the rising backwash of the past. I am
nearly weightless now, so thin
    any small arms might encircle me,
my body grown so light I can easily slip
    across the beckoning rim.

Three

Three Poems for Judi

1. FIRST SIGN

Day after day, the fecund, mis-shaped cells
doubled and re-doubled inside her, infused
her blood's unguarded channels and spawned their rank
tumors, unmaking each tissue-woven host—
her left lung first, then her brain, then her spine and bones,
brute Vandals at the marrow. For weeks, or months
(the doctors know so little), she felt nothing,
until that morning in August, a special class

for teachers, when her hand refused to move
or hold her pen, and curled limp against her paper,
a small, stunned thing. It seemed, she said, so strange,
and yet familiar, too, like that scene from a thousand
old westerns: the dozing scout startled to a fury
of dust, the first, faint sounds of horses approaching.

2. THE NONSELF: SOME THINGS
SHE SAID TO ME

*In cancer, non-intelligent cells are multiplying and you are being replaced by the non-you.
Immunologists class the body's cancer cells as 'nonself.'*
—Susan Sontag, Illness as Metaphor

This is Hell, J. says from her hospital bed, *and I
don't mean Hell, I mean Hell.* Like a comic
lush, she slurs her words, Atavan and morphine
swelling her tongue. Pupils shrunk to motes.

Bald now beneath her cotton turban, sparrow
thin, her body's soft tissues devoured by cancer,
she seems some third sex, the *nonself* the doctors
speak of. Outside, the leaves burn rust and gold,

brighten as they fall against an indifferent sky.
She crooks a finger I can almost see
through, hisses: *She wants to kill me. She's crazy,*
that nurse. You think I'm crazy, but she's

the one. I want to go home. I want to walk
again. Why won't you take me home? You don't know
what it's like. You don't know what this pain is like.
You're putting this in your next book, aren't you—

3. MEETING THE ANGEL

Not as a bird with twelve black wings and an eye
and a tongue for each of us. (Someone dies
each time he blinks.) And not shrouded in celestial
light, a fair-haired castrato. Not as Samael,
angel of poison, his venomous sword quivering
above the parched, open mouths of the dying.
He did not come as Azrael, *whom God helps,*
bearing apples so sweet their fragrance kills
our fear of leaving this known world. What did we
know of death, of suffering? Each day for weeks
we drove the autumn highway to the clinic,
where the angel's rough map ablated J.'s skin
with the blue tattoos of radiology, black
dissolve of surgical stitches. And like, or unlike
God, he was always with us, among the lush,
ongoing trees, the small mercies of fresh
air and afternoon light leavening the cracked
glass, our hearts' stutter, as we reached the exit.

The Life You Really Have

. . . the trees are trying to tell me things I don't want to hear.
  —Richard Jackson

These days each thing speaks
to you, but their languages, thank God,
are untranslatable.
Its voice vaguely sinister,
as if it were about to laugh,
your house murmurs
something about quiet and safety.
Even carpeting, thick as the despair

of the middle class,
can't muffle its whisper.
It's not like those voices K.
heard, fabulous shapes in the air
calling her towards a rope,
the kitchen chair turned over. She heard
the dial tone hiss like a rattler,
woke to Thorazine, restraint. No,

it's more the hum of traffic
and conversation you hear on certain
afternoons, standing on some corner,
maybe in front of the library,
the post office, how each sound
swells into a moment when you don't know
who you are. You're just a woman
standing on the street,

listening to the trees, the day
sunny, or not. You're wearing what
you're wearing, your hair is how it is,
and when you look down

to see the shape of your body,
the particular angle of your shadow or
its absence, everything adds up
to someone familiar who

could be anyone, have any
of those lives you didn't choose—
another man. Or no man.
And possibly it's the sound
of laughter, after all, the audience
a little drunk and sorrowful,
the ancient joke
you finally understand.

Memory from Childhood

after Machado

High summer and the unforgiving
noon sun boils the blacktop. Monotony
of wind, flung grit assaulting
our eyes and ears through the open

car windows. We are escaping Brooklyn.
Behind dark glasses, my mother wrestles the un-
wieldy, ink-stained map. My father smokes
and speeds, watches for patrolmen. Ash

stars from his Luckies stream past my face,
my bare legs stick to vinyl. I'm dreaming
someplace green and cool, imagining
my father won't detour to the dog track,

my mother's face unfrowned. I am pretending
the place we are headed is not where
we are going, even though I know I am
wrong. High summer and the unforgiving

noon sun boils the blacktop. Monotony
of wind, flung grit assaulting
our eyes and ears through the open
car windows. We are escaping Brooklyn.

Luminous Child

The patient will not speak
except to say *tomato, broom, fire.*
Anger appears to be a major issue in this case.
Mother's history reveals
a fascination with certain wrong-way
streets, the rumpled sheets
of backroom cots, an edgy desire
for loss common to compulsive
gamblers. Patient manifests an obsessive
fantasy concerning *the dark lakes*
of Peru, where in dreams
he's a white light, a bullet
plunging deep through water the red sheen
of Beaujolais. He's an infant,
pearly and round, tracing the rapid
downshift of a freefall no mother
can catch. Patient denies
any memory of riding through November
yellows, Dallas, the back
of his mother's bike, sipping air
sweet with lilac, speed
carrying them both through streets
blurred with color, her hair windy
and soft in his face, the familiar arc
of her neck and back between him
and whatever came on. He would like
to confess the theft of his
mother's pearl ring, gift for a girl
whose hair kinked and roiled
like Janis Joplin's in the photograph
on his mother's album, Big Brother
and the Holding Co., like bikers, his gone
father, he thinks. He can no more
explain his need than that luminous child
spiraling through Peruvian dream
waters can explain his, or you, yours.
Me, mine.

Flying West

1

Lifting off from Kennedy,
swaddled in this mist's fine scrim,
my plane banks east
over darkening slabs and ledges,
slick basalt, the icy,
brackish waters of my childhood.
The moon's a flat wafer
signaling *slow* as we circle
west for Wright's Ohio.

2

Beneath the river continuously
losing itself, engulfed
somewhere I can't see by this vast,
salty surge, the graffiti-
less cars of the '65 IRT still bear
my sad father back from the city,
its glamour fallen from him,
shaken dust. He's reading
the *Post*—*Giants 24, Packers 17*—
one arm rocking gently
in the traction of a frayed strap.
He's slender as a boy.
The day's scheme of circles
and lines not yet permanently carved
on his face.

3

I try to sleep, call up
from the ochre light pooling
on my companion's novel
our kitchen's winter yellow, my mother
humming over fried potatoes,
cracked Melmac the color
of some nauseous sea, dimestore
glasses set for four.
The Edge of Night sends its strings
and quarrels across the hall.
Is she thinking of the sketch
she's left half-finished,
a hasty charcoal rose?

Art

. . . ordinary isn't possible anymore
　—Adam Zagajewski

In the teachers' lounge, the tall, pretty
Irish woman tells me her anorexic
daughter's been hospitalized two years.
She's fifteen. Their debts are something she can
only laugh about. I sip tepid coffee,
tell her about the afternoon I watched
deputies cuff my son, pat him down
against a black and white while he invited
them to *"suck my cock, fuck"* him *"in the ass"*
and cried. Today, I teach figurative
constructions to high school juniors signed up
for creative writing in hope of an easy grade.
I quote Wallace Stevens, wonder
what metaphor I can use to find the unities
in this: what was he "like" raging by that car?
Was the sun "fiery"? The police faces
"stone"? Soon, I'll speak to English teachers
from four schools about the value of "art
and imagination" to students whose twelve-step
stories of locked wards and halfway-house
failures I've listened to all week.
I don't know what to say about these stories,
how to explain that they come to me daily,
as if I wear some sign. And I don't know
what it means, as I watch them laughing
in school hallways, slamming their lockers,
tonguing each other in a sweet approximation
of love. When I call him at the hospital,
my son tells me a story: a friend
has died, the rumor is someone scotchgarded
his dope. Forgive me if this seems
extreme—I don't know how to make things
ordinary anymore, though I dress and go to work

each day as if the world were ordinary,
as if our lives might unfurl easily as some
well-mannered plot—carefully
rounded characters strolling bucolic paths,
safe beneath lucid trees, their steps
measured and graceful as the orderly
progression of their lives—a shapeliness
such as no one might imagine anymore.

Ode for My Son at Seventeen

Insensible as a river stone to the chill
currents that ferry it above the water's
roughly turning bed, you drift, slack-jawed,
along the needle's curving stream, legal
narcotics closing the bright circuit of your blood.
Alone in the waiting room's submarine light,
two achromatic landscapes and the placid
thrum of Muzak for company, I check
the time too often, try to forget what I've read—
how some believe that anaesthesia steals
the soul. *Without esthetic,* it means you can't feel
and won't recall whatever dreams abrade
your false sleep. My friend D. says, *Life's trouble.*

*Children make us bigger targets for God's
malice.* I fear my own unquiet dreams of those
lost to accident or fate: the overdosed
and near-drowned, the scalded, their nodding heads
like great, dumb peonies. Those who don't recognize
their names anymore, who've forgotten how
to grasp a fork. I fear the terrible bland prose
of the waiver I've just signed: *I disavow
any right to damages. Rare side effects may
include a slowed heart rate, a drop in blood
pressure, coma, and death.* I shake my head
no to the blonde receptionist's sour coffee,
no to these wild imaginings I've conjured

from what I know is nothing, or close.
The nurse arrives: you'll wake up soon.
As if they were the final moments
in some rare, mesmeric film, its end
impossible to guess, I watch
each lucky minute round the clock.

Half-Light: No Feeling

And then winter, chill light
fading with the afternoon, the various greys
deepening to violet and charcoal
beyond the steam-clouded pane.
Her tea cooling in a chipped, enamelled mug,

a young woman sits listening
to the voice of a man she once loved
swearing grief's whitened his hair
in the year since she left him, that he longs
for their child. The first streetlights

hum on and all along the block,
the tranquil glow of shuttered houses
in their yellow hoops of porchlight,
as if nothing within could ever be too wrong.
Now the man weeps, he wants her

to come someplace he calls home, but she
wants only to forget him, which is why
she has travelled so far, leaving miles
of prairie and complicated highways,
the endless small towns, and filthy, dazzling

cities, those hundreds of thousands
of strangers, between them. I was that woman,
and nights like this, blues on the radio
and ice stippling every window, I try
to understand what love is, how it disappears

and leaves us strange to those once
ached for. Only images return: a flowered
cup on a sill, the early December dark.
A once-cherished voice, grown distant
as the moon. No feeling I can begin to name.

Sometimes When You're Asleep

and I'm counting the regular pulse
of the motel sign, its hothouse-
    flower vermilion splashed
on the musky rug, I remember the man

and woman I watched walking
    together under cottonwoods tall
and thick around as ancient
    columns, not touching, the absence
of touch somehow palpable

between them, I thought.
    It was one of those April days so blue
the sky seems lacquered,
    and I could hear jays and music
drifting past from the transistor radios

of children playing hookey.
    I thought they were probably in love,
though he was much younger,
    and only she wore a ring. I want
to wake you when I remember

how they stopped on a slight
    rise to watch as two grey-winged hawks
described an ellipse above the top
    branches, their paths cutting
across the sun. To ask if you believe,

as I do, that as they stood
    there, the woman squinting beneath
a shielding hand, the man's
    eyes behind dark glasses, the radiant
warmth of afternoon through their light

jackets, that it must have
    been for them a moment that even now
they remember, one of those days
    when you want so much you want nothing
and everything isn't enough.

Heat

This isn't, I swear,
    another love poem, though I confess
        I'm feeling sultry

as an Alabama belle. *This heat*—
    102 degrees for days, for weeks
        no rain, air so heavy

with its need to pour,
    paper on my desk curls, damp.
        Enervating as the Santa Ana

in some *noir* film, wind
    fevers the trees, the black
        and white moment

just before some grade-B
    actor, sweating through his sharkskin
        jacket, is strangled

or shot, or the tough-guy
    detective sets his shot glass,
        rim sweating, too,

on the bar to order another.
    It's the wind that knocks wildly
        against the kitchen window

as he makes love to a rich
    man's wife—*red nails, gold ankle
        bracelet*—on a blessedly

cool tile floor. At my desk,
    I move in slow motion, clothes
        sticking. And yes, when

I press its matte surface
   to my face, your photo cools my skin.
      We'd be like those lovers,

deaf to the prelude
   of sirens, her husband's
      key in the lock.

Georgic on Waking

At the hour when the last streetlight
dims, resuming its dull face,
and the sky pales into the arcing
blues or greys you recognize
as morning, swim up slowly, careful
diver, and release, as you rise,
whatever catch you've netted.
Loosen the silky sein of your dreams,
its freight of skittering, rapid-eye
fish with their now-bright, now-murky
scales, their quick-darting fins,
night's shape-shifting images of *memory*
and desire receding as you surface.
Lie still until each shadowed corner
and shrouded, somehow unfamiliar,
object inhabiting your room assumes
the known geometries of daylight.
If alone, depend upon whatever sounds
honeycomb your window: a racket
of birds turfing out to the rhythm
of boot heels scuffling gravel, far trucks
downshifting, their hundred clearing
throats; on the good musk escaping
your skin, tart scent of sweat and lemon.
If good fortune's left its elusive mark,
the small heat of a lover's breath
beside you, count yourself lucky.
Let him sleep, but move against him,
until each pulsing curve and sheltering
angle fits completely. Let him sleep,
as you rest your palm beneath
whatever warms him, the antenna
of your fingertips light above his signaling
heart. Then speak that language
you knew before you knew language,
before you had to learn day's difficult
vocabulary, that yammering patois.

Pigeons furl the silk of their oilslick
   wings and doze on the limed shoulders
      of forgotten generals, while the last

commuters descend to the subways,
   where they'll sway above their papers,
      reflections streaming through the rapid

dark. Christened *bleue* by the French,
   this is the hour when evening raises
      its azure wand and the light smolders,

cool center of a candle flame,
   the five ring on an archer's target,
      a few stars the silvery nibs of arrows

just breaking through. Slender boys
   in waiters' tuxes snap starched linens
      over tables for two, as cabbies scour

backseats clean of the day's real
   detritus, and one by one, all over
      the city, vapor lamps spread their sodium

veils like some fast-traveling rumor,
   gild the drowsing streets, graffitied
      buildings, until even the harbor, the river

freighted with sludge, even the smoke-
   stacks percolating a foul snow of ash
      and grit over the Jersey Palisades,

have gone soft-focus, the whole town
   a Chamber of Commerce photo or moony
      perfume ad. Prelude to the strict black

of night, this is the moment we may
    imagine the hiss of nylon, the garter
        a woman slides, high on her leg,

for a man dressing, even now, in his best
    suit, when we find ourselves humming
        Gershwin tunes, thinking *romance*,

possibility—of glamour we know better
    than by day. Which is why the woman
        lingers, her heart beating like a bird's

does, too quickly, why the man hesitates
    beneath her window, his face chiaroscuro
        in blue shadow, a square of light.

Grace

From the next-door court, the echoing
   sounds of a game, pick-up basketball,
men shouting, and the sweet, rocking
   harmonies of "I Second That Emotion,"

amped up loud and slightly tinny
   on a cheap cassette, joyous all the same.
Someone, mercifully, has killed
   the fluorescent overheads and lifted

the shades, and now this small gym
   floats in a dazzle of sunlight,
our repeating images, sweat-suited women
   and men, my own glistening skin,

lost in the brilliant glare
   reflecting off the mirrored wall.
There is no other world than this one,
   I believe it. Simple enough

to conjure metaphor—stasis,
   entrapment—from this rote walk
to nowhere, this treadmill with its queer,
   spongy belt endlessly cycling,

pale numbers for time passed,
   for distance traveled only
in the digital imagination of its computer,
   pulsing calmly through the black sheen

of its blind face—me,
   panting to slim my forty-year-old body,
toughen my aging heart. But this morning,
   I can almost believe anything

is possible; this world,
    with its intricate and mutable
geographies, so many restless
    players weaving the extraordinary

stories of their lives,
    is enough. I'm not saying it's more
than this luminous September sky,
    a feeling transitory as the good

chill through our window,
    where hours ago, I woke to solace,
the small heat of your breath
    against my arm. Or that night's

relentless ghosts won't return
    to lead me, a dim and anxious student
of the cold, planetary dark,
    to that same window, unable to sleep.

Still, how lavish, even this
    momentary knowing, the past dissolving
to muscle and pulse, the autumn
    morning, this music filtering through.

Florigraphy

Because it is your wedding day,
we surround you

and ourselves with custom's
fragrant alphabet,

this dazzling floral lexicon
of our good wishes

blossoming among pews,
signifying faithfulness

and long life, love everlasting,
from each pinned lapel,

each *tussie mussie* chorusing
from our hands, the natural voices

of peonies and baby's breath,
sweet William, so beloved

by the Victorians, each animate
bloom herald of our best

ambitions. But we who spend
our days crafting what we can

of plainer language must hedge
our bets against what's perishable,

and so I offer you this small bouquet,
less brightly hued but, with luck,

more lasting, a botany of words
to fix my fondest hopes—

Violet for love, life's sweetness.
For passion, the Rose.
Marjorum for joy, Ivy for friendship.
Eglantine, the poet's flower.
This prayer that your lives together
Will flourish, brilliant
As this chapel's hothouse vocabulary,
Your love last as long
As the ineluctable made music
Of our words to name them.

Prayer

For skies bleaching like sheets in late August,
virgin olive oil blessed by garlic,
                    chocolate and oranges, your name
          in my mouth. For the upcountry buzz
of a motorcycle, lace spray
          of the gravel, the sound of a fiddle,
Gershwin, or Patsy Cline.
For the open-mouthed sleepers who dream floating
          bridges, sleep dreamless as death,
              if death is peaceful. For girls
      with razor-cut hair working at K-Mart and Shopko
          clothed in their holy boredom,
and for the graceful boys who linger outside,
      posing. For Virginia rose and china cockle, purple
              vetch clinging beside the Atlantic, each
          constellation exploding invisibly
      above the overlit city. For last night's fingers of rain,
          the leaves stripped
      from the sugar maple, the way they pressed
themselves against the sidewalk, fragrant and dark
          as roses crushed in a book.

"White Cat and Notebook: A Still Life" is dedicated, with love and gratitude, to the memory of the late Lynda Hull (1954–1994).

Quotes and research into the life of Van Gogh used in "Contrast, Composition" are drawn from *The Letters of Vincent Van Gogh*, edited by Mark Roskill.

The film referenced in "Kiss" is *First Knight*, a recent retelling of the Camelot legend.

The title "For the Dark Girl" refers to a particularly self-lacerating poem of Parker's, "The Dark Girl's Rhyme." For research into Parker's life, I drew upon Marion Meade's excellent biography, *Dorothy Parker: What Fresh Hell Is This*.

"Triptych: For Michael" is for the painter Michael David.

"In the Frame" is for Edith Singer.

"Far Rockaway" is for Edward Singer.

"Debut: Late Lines for a Thirtieth Birthday" is for Erin Belieu.

"Against Romance" is for Betsy Sholl.

"Muse" is for Carol-Lynn Marrazzo; for my research into the life of Vivienne Eliot, I relied primarily on Michael Hasting's fine play, *Tom & Viv*, and three excellent biographies of T. S. Eliot—Peter Ackroyd's *Eliot* and Lyndall Gordon's *Eliot's Early Years* and *Eliot's New Life*.

"Three Poems for Judi" is in memory of Judi Aizenberg Lerner (1947–1998).

"Luminous Child" is for Christopher Aizenberg.

"Ode for My Son at Seventeen" is for Aaron Aizenberg.

"Grace" is for Jeffrey Aizenberg.

"Florigraphy" is for Erin Belieu and Jeremy Countryman. My research into the Victorian language of flowers is drawn from Kathleen Gips's lovely book *Flora's Dictionary: The Victorian Language of Herbs and Flowers.*

This Country of Mothers
Julianna Baggott

In Search of the Great Dead
Richard Cecil

Names above Houses
Oliver de la Paz

The Star-Spangled Banner
Denise Duhamel

Winter Amnesties
Elton Glaser

Fabulae
Joy Katz

Train to Agra
Vandana Khanna

Crossroads and Unholy Water
Marilene Phipps

Misery Prefigured
J. Allyn Rosser